SUCCEEDING WITH THE MASTERS™

CLASSICAL ERA, Volume Two

Compiled and edited by Helen Marlais

About the Series

Succeeding with the Masters™ is a series dedicated to the authentic keyboard works of the Baroque, Classical, Romantic, and Twentieth-Century masters.

This series provides a complete and easily accessible method for learning and performing the works of the masters. Each book presents the works in historical perspective for the student, and provides the means and the motivation to play these pieces in the correct stylistic, musical, and technical manner. The easily understandable format of practice strategies and musical concepts makes this series enjoyable to both students and teachers.

To ensure authenticity, all of these pieces have been extensively researched. Teachers will find a wealth of excellent repertoire that can be used for recitals, festivals, competitions, and state achievement testing. Many of these original compositions may be new to you while others will be familiar. This series brings together an essential and comprehensive library of the pedagogical repertoire of the great composers.

Succeeding with the Masters™ begins with late-elementary repertoire, continues through intermediate-level works and also includes a few early-advanced works. Upon completion of this series, students will be well prepared for the entry-level sonatas by the master composers.

THE
F·J·H
MUSIC
COMPANY
INC.

Production: Frank and Gail Hackinson
Production Coordinators: Philip Groeber and Isabel Otero Bowen
Cover: Terpstra Design, San Francisco
Text Design and Layout: Susan Pinkerton
Engraving: Tempo Music Press, Inc.
Printer: Tempo Music Press, Inc.

ISBN 1-56939-390-7

PREFACE

A Note for Teachers and Students

Succeeding with the Masters™, Classical Era Volume Two, continues the collection of graded repertoire featuring the great masters of the Classical era. Volume Two includes intermediate-level pieces and a few early-advanced pieces. This collection of marvelous repertoire builds a foundation for playing advanced classical music. After studying and performing these pieces, the student will be ready for the entry-level sonatas by these composers. As a guide to practicing the piano works of Haydn, Mozart, and Beethoven, each piece is introduced with a short "discovery" of a particular characteristic of the Classical era. Brief segments on "practice strategies" and "musical concepts" guide the student in how to prepare and perform the piece. Students can use these concepts as valuable resources when learning all classical repertoire pieces.

Two icons are used throughout the volume:

Characteristics of the Classical Era

indicates the Musical Characteristics of the Classical era

Practice Strategy

outlines a Practice Strategy or illustrates a musical concept that guides the student in how to learn more efficiently and play more musically.

Many published collections take great liberties in altering pitches, rhythms, and articulations that the composers clearly did not intend. The pieces in this collection, however, are based on Urtext editions, which are editions that reflect the composer's original intent. From these Urtext scores, the editor has created a performance score for the student.

- Fingerings have been added by the editor.
- Articulations and dynamic markings have been added in some cases to guide the students as they explore the classical style.
- Editorial metronome markings are added as a guide.
- Ornaments have been realized for the student and are seen as ossias above the staff.
- The CD includes complete performances and a practice strategy workshop. For a complete listing of track numbers, see page six.

MUSIC DURING THE CLASSICAL ERA (1750–1820)

The music of Haydn, Mozart, and Beethoven was heard mainly in courts of kings and queens across Europe or in homes and town gathering places. Wealthy nobility such as Prince Lobkowitz and Count Razumovsky, two of Beethoven's patrons, had concert halls within their very own palaces, and other wealthy private home owners would open their homes to performers who were traveling throughout Europe.

As compared to the piano music of the Romantic era, classical composers of piano music did not supply titles that cause us to imagine a particular visual image or story. Rather, pieces were named according to function, such as "German Dance," "Country Dance," and "Minuet."

During the Classical era, Vienna was the musical center of Europe. Composers and musicians came to this city to live and work. The composers of the Classical period reacted against the grandeur and complexity of the Baroque style. Although the style was on the surface simple and more direct, the Classical era was a time of innovation, especially in the area of form. Theme and variations, rondo, and sonata form were all relatively new, as well as the genres of piano sonatas, piano concertos, the symphony, and string quartet. This was the age of classical orchestras as well.

MUSICAL CHARACTERISTICS OF THE CLASSICAL ERA:

- Melodies are elegant, graceful, and oftentimes easy to sing.
- Simple, flowing melodies move to predictable cadences.
- Phrases are well-balanced and symmetrical.
- Classical forms are balanced and symmetrical: binary, rounded binary, ternary (such as a minuet and trio), rondo, theme and variations, and sonata form.
- Ornamentation is used, but in a simpler style than in the Baroque (trills, trills with terminations, mordents, *appoggiaturas*, turns).
- Short and repetitive melodic motives combine to form phrases.
- Homophonic texture is prevalent (a clear melody in the right hand, with an accompaniment in the left hand).
- Straightforward, simple harmonies are used (primary chords).
- There is often a "contrast of mood," as compared to only one mood felt in the works of the Baroque period.
- Rhythmic motives are varied.
- Dynamic changes are prevalent and contribute to the overall expression of the piece.

THE REPERTOIRE IN THIS VOLUME

The pieces in Volume Two display a wide range of character as well as emotion. You will encounter the dance pieces of the era, such as minuets and trios, with their binary forms (see Volume One for more details), as well as a Gypsy Dance and a Waltz, a set of Theme and Variations, a Bagatelle and an Allemande, a Funeral March, the famous *Für Elise*, and even a piece for a glass harmonica!

The emphasis during the Classical era in music, art, and architecture was on simplicity, balance, and symmetry. Can you see those elements in this picture?

Typical Italian design for a building
incorporating Classical features

What the student will learn in Volume Two:

Characteristics of the era:

HAYDN PIECES:

MOZART PIECES:

BEETHOVEN PIECES:

Practice strategies:

Volume Two – Intermediate/Early Advanced Repertoire

The pieces within each composer category are arranged in order of difficulty, with the least difficult pieces immediately following the short biography of the composer.

For a complete list of sources for these pieces, see page 102.

FRANZ JOSEPH HAYDN

(1732–1809)

Franz Joseph Haydn was employed by a noble Hungarian family by the name of Esterházy. They were great patrons of the arts. Haydn worked for them for 48 years. Today the great palace of Esterháza can be found in the western side of Hungary in Europe, which, in Haydn's day, was part of the Austro-Hungarian Empire. When the Esterházys wanted to display their good taste and wealth, they would invite foreigners to hear and see music being made in their very own opera house, theatre, or two concert halls. Imagine staying in one of their 126 guest rooms for one of these events! Haydn's permanent position with the Esterházys as a composer was a notable accomplishment in itself, but he worked practically non-stop, because his job was not only to compose music, but to have it performed any time the Prince asked. He was in charge of all of the musicians in the orchestra, the singers in the operas, all of the instruments, and all of the performers' attire. And, he composed every day! Haydn wrote of his life:

> My prince [Nicholas] was pleased with all my work, I was commended,
> and as conductor of an orchestra I could make experiments, observe
> what strengthened and what weakened an effect and thereupon improve,
> substitute, omit, and try new things; I was cut off from the world, there
> was no one around to mislead and harass me, and so I was forced to
> become original.[1]

Haydn is considered the "father of the symphony." He wrote 104 of them, developing a genre that would inspire composers for generations to come. He perfected the form and gave the symphony status in society. He added a charming minuet and trio as one of the movements, he developed themes as no one had done before, and he often added theme and variations as the slow movement. His finales (fourth movements) were robust and cheerful.

Haydn wrote music that was symmetrical in form with a human touch, allowing for lyrical expression and emotion. Much of his music is happy in character, expressing his affectionate and spontaneous personality.

Portrait of Haydn from a painting by
Ludwig Guttenbrunn, c.1780

To learn more about Haydn, turn to page 16.

[1] Donald Jay Grout, editor. A History of Western Music. W.W. Norton and Company, Inc. New York, New York, 1973, p. 478.

Minuet in D major

From a collection entitled 18 Menuette und Aria in F per il Clavicembalo

**Characteristics
of the
Classical Era**

The form of a minuet and trio:

Minuet	Trio	Minuet
A	B	A
aabb	ccdd	ab

Both the minuet and the trio have two repeated sections. At the close of the trio section, the words *da capo* tell us to return to "the head" or beginning. So we go back and play the minuet again, this time *without* repeats.

If we look at the minuet section by itself we see that it follows **BINARY** form:

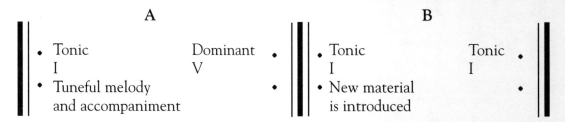

A

- Tonic   Dominant
  I   V
- Tuneful melody
  and accompaniment

B

- Tonic   Tonic
  I   I
- New material
  is introduced

This is an example of a slight variation on the typical binary form. Usually the B section begins on the dominant, whereas in this piece it begins on tonic.

(For background information on the minuet and trio, see Volume One, Classical Era.)

**Practice
Strategy**

Practicing ornaments:

In the Classical era, composers wrote ornaments into their music to embellish the sound. An ornament is like frosting on a cake—it is used to decorate, and to make the whole cake, or piece of music, more grand.

First, learn this minuet and trio without the ornaments. When you are sure that you can play this minuet at a steady tempo, then you are ready to add the finishing touches.

The two different ornaments you can play in this Minuet are the *trill* and the *mordent*.

In the Classical era, performers usually ended trills with terminations. This means the performer played a lower neighbor and then the principal note (see the example below).

The trill: ✶✶ or *tr*   trill with termination:

All trills begin on the beat, and in the Baroque and Classical eras, they begin on the upper note.[1]

The mordent:

The mordent is always played on the beat, starting on the main note. This three-note embellishment begins on the principal note, goes down, and then back up. Play the mordent cleanly and rapidly. Mordents are often used in ascending melodic lines, such as from measure 26-30 in the trio section. The mordents in this piece are editorial.

Balancing the melody with the accompaniment:

The left hand actually plays more notes than the right hand, but the right-hand melody must project out over the left-hand accompaniment.

In order to balance the right hand *over* the left, practice in the following two ways to hear the difference in dynamics:

1) Play the left hand much *louder* than the right hand, feeling more weight from your arm and hand going to the bottom of the keys.
2) Next, play the right hand much *louder* than the left hand, again feeling more weight from your arm and hand going to the bottom of the keys. Listen for the phrase goal. (The phrase goal is the place the music naturally moves toward; after arrival at its goal, the phrase naturally tapers.)

Does the piece sound better with a louder right hand or left hand? If you are playing it correctly, projecting the right-hand melody over the left hand is the sound and approach you want to take for the entire piece.

Practice Strategy

▔ or ▪̣

Several places in this piece you will notice *tenuto* markings above notes that are to be played *staccato*. This means you will play these notes their full value, but detached. Listen to the recording to hear these articulations.

Practice Strategy

---

[1]C.P.E. Bach (one of J.S. Bach's sons), wrote an *Essay on the True Art of Playing Keyboard Instruments* that explained how keyboard instruments were played during the Classical era. His instructions for ornamentation were learned from his father.

MINUET IN D MAJOR

Franz Joseph Haydn
Hob. IX: 20, No. 1

(a) Optional trill:

N.B. The longer slurs have been added to show the shape of the phrase.
* Students may choose to play a mordent or a trill in measures 26 and 30,
according to the performance practice of the day.

MINUET IN B FLAT MAJOR

This piece is part of a set of minuets, probably used as teaching repertoire as well as a study for Haydn's larger orchestral and string quartet works.

Well-balanced and symmetrical four-measure phrases:

Mark in your score the four-bar phrases and notice how the simple, flowing melodies move to predictable cadences, such as I ⇨ V⁷ (measures 6-8, A section) and then V⁷ ⇨ I at the end of the minuet (measures 15 and 16, B section).

"Blocking" is a practice strategy you can use for many repertoire pieces.

The term refers to the practice of grouping melody notes into chords or intervals.

Playing the melody notes in *harmonic* formation helps you see and feel the patterns of a piece more quickly than if you tried to learn the piece without using the blocking strategy.

Melodic notes of a
B flat major chord

Same notes, blocked in
harmonic formation.

Measures 1-8 from the Minuet:

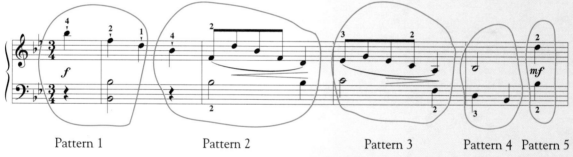

Pattern 1   Pattern 2   Pattern 3   Pattern 4   Pattern 5

Pattern 6   Pattern 7   Pattern 8   Pattern 9   Pattern 10

Shown below are the exact eight measures, this time in condensed form with all of the patterns *blocked*. Practice these blocked patterns until you feel secure with them. Then try blocking other harmonic patterns of the piece!

B♭ major (I)   B♭ major (I)   F major (V7)   B♭ major (I)   vii°⁶₅   vii°⁴₃/V   V⁶   V/V   V

Practicing forwards as well as backwards:

Since music is created in patterns, practice the following *arpeggio* and broken chord patterns found in the minuet.

Use the following metronome speeds:

Eighth note ♪ = M.M. 88, 100, and 152.
Quarter note ♩ = M.M. 120 and 132.

Repeating the patterns many times will help your fingers remember them, and you will learn the piece quickly!

Pick up to measure 1:
a)

becomes:

measure 2:
b)

becomes:

measure 3:
c)

becomes:

measure 6:
d)

becomes:

Find these four patterns in your score.
Choose several other motivic patterns in the minuet to practice forwards and backwards.

Minuet in B flat major

Franz Joseph Haydn
Hob. IX: 20, No. 3

(a) For additional trill information, see page eight.

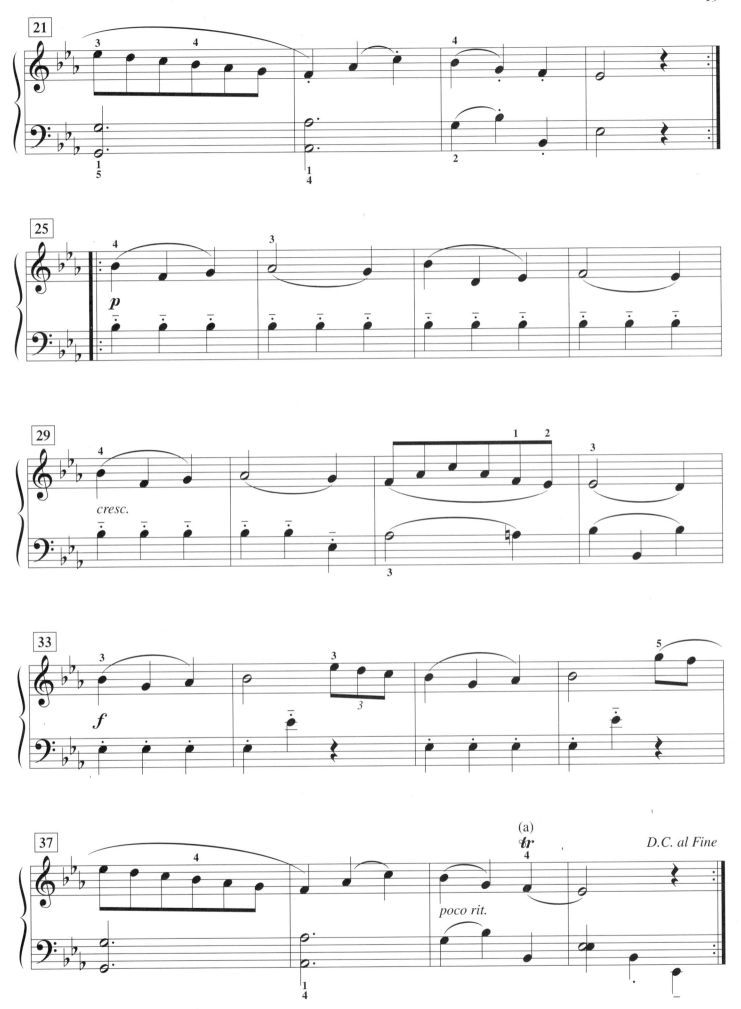

N.B. Listen to the recording to hear how mordents are used to decorate on the repeats.

MORE ABOUT FRANZ JOSEPH HAYDN

Haydn wrote in a letter about his own work:

> Often, when I was wrestling with all kinds of difficulties which
> impeded my art, a secret feeling whispered to me: perhaps (your)
> work may now and then become a spring from which the man
> who is careworn or overburdened with occupations can draw rest
> and refreshment for a few moments.[2]

Haydn also played an important role in the development of the string quartet. Mozart dedicated his last six string quartets to Haydn in respect and recognition of Haydn's influence over the genre. The symphony, the string quartet, and the sonata were all developments of the Classical era.

Haydn composed and conducted symphonies for audiences in London, England, which gave him two opportunities to experience life beyond Esterháza. He wrote two great oratorios toward the end of his life (*The Creation* and *The Seasons*), and spent his last years comfortably. His creative output was massive — nearly 890 instrumental works which include his piano compositions, symphonies, and string quartets. He also wrote eighteen operas, fourteen masses, three oratorios, and about 620 songs.

A Dutch collector of music named Anthony van Hoboken researched and assigned each work a number, now called the Hoboken number, which is why each piece is followed by the abbreviation, "Hob."

[2]Hans Gall. <u>The Musician's World – Letters of the great composers</u>.
Thames and Hudson. London, England, 1978, p. 66.

The Palace at Esterháza in the 1700s

GYPSY DANCE IN C MAJOR

This dance is from a collection entitled, *Zingarese für Klavier*.
Translated, *Zingarese für Klavier* means, "Gypsy Dances for Keyboard."

Characteristics of the Classical era exemplified in this lively and highly spirited piece:

- Balanced and symmetrical forms
  This piece is in minuet and trio form, with the trio section in *minor*.
- Homophonic texture permeates the piece
- "Contrast of mood" between the minuet and the trio sections
- Varied rhythmic motives
- Simple harmonies throughout

**Characteristics
of the
Classical Era**

In classical music, the tonic and dominant chords are the most important.

The dominant chord is the same in major and in minor, but the tonic chord sounds different in major than in minor.

**Characteristics
of the
Classical Era**

Listen to the *Gypsy Dance* on the recording and hear how the minor section sounds different. We use a big Roman numeral for major (I), and a little Roman numeral to identify minor (i). Circle in your score the major I chords, and then circle the minor i chords. Label all of the dominant chords as Roman numeral V.

MAJOR:

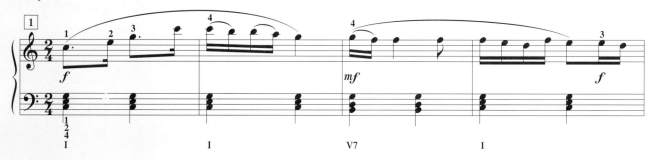

MINOR:

GYPSY DANCE IN C MAJOR

Franz Joseph Haydn
Hob. IX: 28, No. 1

N.B. The longer slurs have been added to show the shape of the phrase.

FF1437

MINUET IN D MAJOR

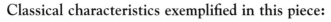

This piece is from a collection entitled *Twelve Minuets*.

Characteristics of the Classical Era

Practice Strategy

Classical characteristics exemplified in this piece:

- Melodies that are elegant, graceful, and easy to sing
- Simple, flowing melodies moving to predictable cadences

Practicing ornaments in classical repertoire:

Appoggiaturas:

In the Classical era, it was common for composers to write *appoggiaturas* as auxiliary notes. The value of the *appoggiatura* should be subtracted from the value of the main note.[1] *Appoggiaturas* start *on the beat*. Use the following guide for all classical repertoire pieces:

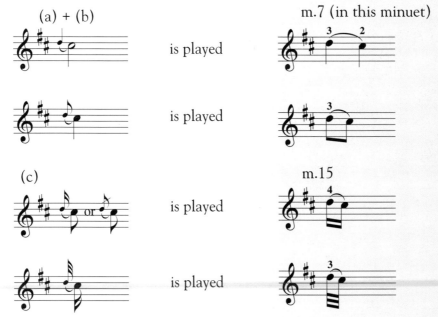

Trills with termination:

During the Classical era, standard trills usually started on the upper auxiliary note, and ended with a turned ending (termination), whether or not the turned ending was actually printed in the piece.

Learn this minuet and trio without any of the ornaments first. Then use this page to isolate and practice only the ornaments. When you feel secure, add the ornaments to the piece.

[1] C.P.E. Bach, *Essay on the True Art of Playing Keyboard Instruments*.

Collegium Musicum concert, 1777; engraving by Rudolf Halzhalb

Minuet in D major

Franz Joseph Haydn
Hob. IX: 3, No. 1

*N.B. Quarter notes should be played slightly detached unless marked otherwise.
The fermatas in measure 12 are editorial.

MINUET IN C MAJOR

This Minuet is from the collection of Twelve Minuets for
the Clavecin or Piano Forte

**Practice
Strategy**

Practicing eighth notes against triplets - "2 against 3":

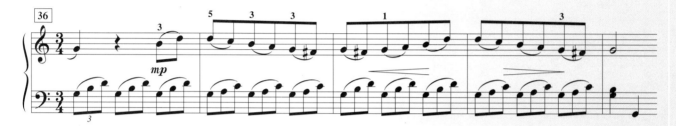

Here is a step-by-step approach to succeed in playing this figure:

1) With the metronome set at a quarter note = M.M. 60,
   tap the rhythm of the right hand:

2) Then **vocalize** the rhythm of the left hand at the same tempo:

Repeat each rhythm several times and then try the next step:

3) Try both lines (1 and 2) at the same time (tapping and vocalizing).

   tap this line while

   vocalizing and tapping this line

4) Then repeat lines 1) and 2) several times again. Then do 3). Stick with it!

5) After several complete sets of 1), 2), and 3), you may try repeating 3).

Once you are secure, increase the tempo with your metronome.

Bringing the piece to life after it is learned:

Listen to the CD recording of this piece and describe this piece with colors. The driving minuet section contrasts with the more gentle, lyrical sentiment of the trio section. Place an "M" after the color below that defines the music of the minuet, and then place a "T" after the color that defines the music of the trio section.

pale blue   *bright red*   *light yellow*

fiery orange   *lustrous brown*   *eggplant purple*

Title page image for the first edition of Haydn's *Trio*, Hob. XV:10, 1798

MINUET IN C MAJOR

Franz Joseph Haydn
Hob. IX: 8, No. 1

(a) Optional trill:

SCHERZO IN F MAJOR

This piece, written in 1772, is from a collection entitled *Pieces for a Musical Clock*. A "musical clock" is an instrument with small pipes arranged horizontally in the base of the clock cabinet.
At the stroke of every hour, one of Haydn's clock pieces would play. The tone quality of these pipes is delicate, so this is the sound you can try to capture when playing this piece on the piano. The Viennese family who owned the original 1789 clock nicknamed the clock *Der Kaffeeklatsch,* or "The Coffee Party," perhaps because the clock chimes signaled to the family members when to have their afternoon coffee party.

Characteristics of the Classical Era

There is a "contrast of mood" in the works of the Classical era:

This Scherzo has a bubbly, energetic character. There are at least three different moods in this piece, which can be likened to varying personalities found in the people who socialized around the table. Listening to the CD, mark in your score (with a pencil!) where you think each section's distinctive mood, or personality, is.

Mood No. 1

lively and **industrious**

Mood No. 2

delightful and sparkling

Mood No. 3

shy and introverted

Practice Strategy

Voicing the melody:

To "voice" a melody means to bring out one of the notes in an interval or chord that is played *within the same hand.* The following practice strategies help you to learn how to voice in either *legato* or *staccato* passages:

Legato two-note slurs:

Measure 14:

Measure 25:

Staccato passages:

Measures 3-5:

Measures 21-24:

To hear the correct voicing, play each beat very slowly, making the top voice's tone bright and *forte*. For the lower voice, make each tone *staccato* and very soft, as shown below. Feel the weight of your arm and hand go to the right side of your hand when you are playing the upper voices.

Measures 25 and 26:

Upper voice bright and full and *forte*

Lower voice *staccato* and *pianissimo*

There are some phrases where the *lower* voices must sing out over the top voices. For example, in measures 19-20, the moving notes in the right hand are much more interesting than the repeated top notes.

To hear the correct voicing, play each beat slowly, making the *lower* voice's tone full and warm. For the *upper* voice, make each tone *staccato* and soft, as shown below. Feel the weight of your arm and hand go to the *left* side of your hand when you are playing with your 1st or 2nd fingers.

Upper voice *staccato* and soft

Lower voice full and warm

Playing repeated notes quickly:

The repeated notes of the left hand in measures 25-30 need to be played quickly and lightly. In order to achieve this goal, change your fingering for each note, like this: 3 2 1 – 3 2 1 – 3 2 1, etc. Play on the tips of your fingers and you will not get tired!

Practice Strategy

Scherzo in F major

Franz Joseph Haydn
Hob. XIX, No. 6

(a) The grace note is played before the beat.

ANDANTE IN G MINOR

This piece was composed as a single movement work, written before 1767. It was not originally intended for the public, but was used as teaching repertoire for Haydn's students.

Characteristics of the Classical Era

This piece exhibits sonata form:

A	B	A
Exposition –	Development –	Recapitulation –
Main theme is presented.	Main theme is developed.	Main theme returns.
Tonic key	Moves away from tonic	Back to tonic

Haydn created this sonata form in minor, so this is the key structure:

Exposition –	Development –	Recapitulation –
KEY: tonic (g minor)	KEY: minor 3rd above tonic (relative major: B flat)	KEY: return to tonic (g minor)

Practice Strategy

Bringing this piece to life:

This piece is introspective. Listening to the CD, mark in your score (with a pencil!) the following interpretive ideas:

1) Mark the overall form in your score (A B A).
   Exposition: measures 1-20.
   Development: pick-up to measure 21 to the middle of measure 41.
   Recapitulation: measure 41, beat four.

2) Mark where you hear the pedal being used.

3) Mark where time is taken (a *rubato* within the phrase, or a *ritardando* at the end of the phrase).

4) Mark the place where the overall sound is "veiled," or very quiet.

5) Mark the one or two phrase goals in each phrase. (Remember, the phrase goal is the place toward which the music naturally moves, and after which it tapers.) Let your ear be your guide and listen to the energy of the melody as it builds toward each goal. From the beginning of the piece to the third beat of measure 2, where is the high point of the phrase? And from the pick-up to measure 3 to the third beat of measure 6, where is the goal of the phrase?

6) Is the theme at the beginning of the recapitulation slightly slower or the same tempo as the exposition?

7) Mark the places that are the loudest.

ANDANTE IN G MINOR

Franz Joseph Haydn
Hob. XVI: 11^{II}

*The *appogiaturas* in this piece are played as two consecutive eighth notes. For example, measure 1 is played:

 (a) Another option:  (c)

PRESTO IN C MAJOR

This piece is also from the collection entitled *Pieces for a Musical Clock* (discussed on page 28). Haydn gave a musical clock instrument, along with many clock pieces, to a family in celebration of their daughter's baptism. The clock can be seen in Vienna, Austria today. When you play this piece, it must sparkle with delicacy.

Characteristics of the Classical Era

Classical melodies are elegant and graceful

Classical melodies are highly repetitive, which means that they are tuneful and easy to recognize and sing. Can you hum the tune of the first eight measures? Singing the melody helps you understand the phrase direction.

Practice Strategy

Slow vs. fast practicing (3 x 1 rule)

It is important to practice slowly as well as *a tempo* in order to be able to perform this piece well. Slow practice locks in the muscle memory and promotes accuracy and security, whereas *a tempo* practice encourages spontaneity, which is exactly what happens in performance.

Using the 3 x 1 rule: practice the segments below by playing them three times slowly (no faster than ♪ = M.M. 112), and then one time, *a tempo* (♪ = M.M. 112). Listen for absolute evenness and clarity in the sixteenths, and do not rush. When you play slowly, play solidly, with a warm, full sound. In order to play quickly and delicately, play very lightly and *piano*.

Segment #1

Segment #2

Measures 38-40:

Measures 40-41:

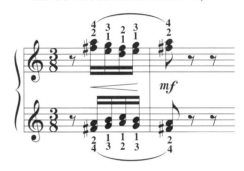

Segment #3

Segment #4

3rd beat of measure 12 to the
third beat of measure 13:

2nd beat of measure 13 to
the downbeat of measure 14:

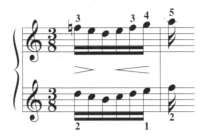

Go ahead and choose other fragments of phrases to try this practice strategy!

A painting commemorating Haydn's 76th birthday, 1808

Presto in C major

Franz Joseph Haydn
Hob. XIX, No. 18

WOLFGANG AMADEUS MOZART

(1756–1791)

Wolfgang Amadeus Mozart's life is a study in contrasts. As a child prodigy, he enjoyed popularity and mirth. Constantly playing concerts for many kings and queens, he was adored. Mozart could listen to a particular piece once and play it back perfectly. He could also immediately improvise a piece in the style of any composer of his day, and the royalty and aristocracy enjoyed watching and listening to this amazing feat. But as he grew older, Mozart's life was much more difficult, and he suffered many hardships. In the 1700s, practically the only way a composer could find stable work was to secure a permanent position with a royal family, and Mozart was never able to secure a position for any length of time. His unfulfilled dream was to find a position in Vienna, the center of all musical activity in all of Europe during his lifetime. For a time, he considered relocating his family to Prague. An excerpt from a letter Franz Joseph Haydn sent to Walter Roth of Prague in 1787, encouraging him to offer Mozart a position there, illustrates Mozart's difficulties.

> If I could but impress the matchless works of Mozart upon the souls
> of all music-lovers, so deeply and with such understanding and
> sensibility as that with which I myself appreciate, and comprehend
> them, the Nations would vie with one another to possess such a
> treasure within their walls. Prague must hold the dear fellow — but
> reward him too; for without that, the history of great geniuses is
> melancholy and gives posterity little encouragement to further effort;
> on which account, alas, so many promising minds fall short of
> fulfillment. It angers me that the peerless Mozart has not yet been
> engaged at an imperial or royal court! Forgive me if I am carried
> away, but I am so fond of the man…[1]

Mozart did not have a permanent position. Instead, he wrote works for many different emperors, most notably Emperor Joseph of Austria and Frederick William of Prussia, and wrote many commissions for court theatres and archbishops. His last work, *The Requiem,* (mass for the dead), was left incomplete. He died young and was buried in a common grave. Mozart's two sons never married, and his wife Constanze remarried but did not have any more children.

Although Constanze had loved her husband very much, she had no idea of his significance until after his death, when people started to make pilgrimages to their home. She then wrote a biography about Mozart, tended to his manuscripts for publishers, and organized benefit concerts of his music. Today, it is hard to believe that a genius of Mozart's magnitude, with such significance in our history, lies forever buried in an unmarked grave.

[1] Hans Gall. The Musician's World – Letters of the great composers. Thames and Hudson. London, England, 1978, p. 60.

Mozart is known as a composer of great operas and for writing forty symphonies, many unrivaled concertos, and much chamber music. By 1775, the *pianoforte* had replaced the harpsichord as the leading keyboard instrument, and Mozart played many concerts on this new instrument. If you visit the Mozart museum in Salzburg, Austria, you can see Mozart's piano, which is two octaves shorter than our modern-day instrument. You will be ready to play his earliest piano sonatas when you have completed this volume, and then later you will be ready for his many variations and piano concertos.

Ludwig Köchel gathered and chronologized all of Mozart's works, which is why each piece has the abbreviation, "K" or "KV."

From an unfinished Mozart portrait by his brother-in-law, Josef Lange, 1782–83

KLAVIERSTÜCK IN F

This "Piano Piece" was written at the beginning of October 1766, in Zürich, Switzerland, when Mozart was ten years old. Elsewhere in the world, England acquired Canada three years earlier.

Characteristics of the Classical Era

Characteristics of the Classical era exemplified in this piece:

- A melody that is elegant, repetitive, and easy to sing
- Phrases that are well-balanced and symmetrical
- Dynamic changes
- Homophonic texture
- Straightforward, simple harmonies

In classical music, the I, IV, and V scale degrees are the most important. In F major, these notes are F (I), B♭ (IV), and C (V). Play each of the following chords based on these scale degrees:

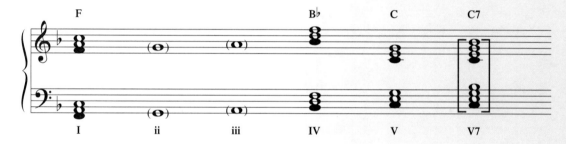

Practice Strategy

Creating a dance-like accompaniment pattern:

The left-hand accompaniment must be perky and light, always providing a supportive framework for the right-hand melody. Think about the last time you saw an Olympic ice skater in action. The skater could jump from the ice and execute a dazzling jump. So it is with our technique at the keyboard — the gravity *away* from the key bed is just as important as dropping our weight into the keys. Up motions are just as important as down motions in piano playing.

In order to play the left-hand accompaniment pattern, drop your wrist and hand to the bottom of the key. Then quickly move your wrist upward and move your whole hand to your thumb. The thumb should play lightly and it should stay close to the keys. Remember never to reach with your fingers, keeping your thumb close to the other fingers of your hand for relaxation.

Klavierstück in F

Wolfgang Amadeus Mozart
KV 33B

* Eighth notes should be played detached (depending on the performer's interpretation).

FF1437

ANDANTE IN F

This piece was probably composed in Brussels, Belgium in
October of 1763, when Mozart was seven years old.

**Practice
Strategy**

Communicating this piece to an audience:
This piece is introspective, gentle, and somewhat melancholy. In order to create this
mood for an audience, the tempo, the touch, and the phrasing must be accurate. Listen
to the recording of this piece, and then experiment with the following musical ideas:

1) The tempo
Experiment with three different tempos for this piece:

♪ = M.M. 100   ♪ = M.M. 48   ♪ = M.M. 72

Always think about creating a forward motion to the line. Which tempo best
characterizes the *Andante* feel?

2) The touch
Slower passages with broken-chord figurations often need some degree of "finger
pedaling" to create a *legatissimo* sound. The right-hand melody can be played clearly over
this accompaniment. Let your left-hand fifth finger hold down the first note longer than
the actual sixteenth-note value of the note.

- Listen to the control in soft and slow passages.

- Listen to your left hand playing quietly, allowing the melody in the
  right hand to be quite sensitive.

- Changing fingering on the same note (measures 24 and 25, for example),
  allows for a taper of the phrase as well as a relaxation gesture.

3) The phrasing
Listen to yourself to make sure that each repetitive phrase has one phrase goal, and that
the end of each phrase tapers in sound. Listening to the recording, circle each phrase
goal in the music. Decide how many short motives create one long phrase, and shape this
entire phrase by thinking of a rounded, clean, flowing manner of playing.

4) The visualization
Create colors in your mind while you listen to this piece and while you play it.
For instance, what color would you choose for measures 1-8?

lavender   *bright yellow*   *forest green*

pink   *autumn gold*   *violet*

ANDANTE IN F

Wolfgang Amadeus Mozart
KV 6

MINUET IN F

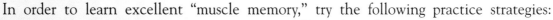

This piece was written on July 16, 1762, in Salzburg. It is likely that
Wolfgang's father, Leopold, wrote the bass line and had his young
six-year-old son complete the melodies to fit the harmonies.

Improving muscle memory:

"Muscle memory" refers to how the muscles in your fingers, hands, wrists, and arms
remember the feel of the keys as each note is played. Your brain sends signals to the
muscles in your body to tell them how to move. If you practice in the correct way, your
muscles will learn much more quickly and you will develop technique that is reliable
even when you are nervous!

**Practice
Strategy**

In order to learn excellent "muscle memory," try the following practice strategies:
1) Divide the piece into four measure segments. Practice with a warm and full sound, and
   play solidly into the keys, with the metronome at the following speeds: ♪ = M.M. 76
   and 92.
2) Next, use **"Impulse" practicing**:

There are three sixteenth-note patterns at both cadential points in this binary form:

**Practice
Strategy**

A Section
Measures 9-10:

B Section
Measures 19-20:

B Section
Measures 21-22:

Four easy steps:

1) Break a phrase into short segments.

   For example, play beats one to two, *a tempo*, listening for evenness. This short segment played quickly, evenly, as well as accurately, is called an "impulse." Play each of these small patterns, or "impulses," quickly, hands separately at first, so that you can feel the gesture in your arms and hands.

2) Then practice beats one to three in the same manner. Listen again for absolute evenness and clarity in the sixteenths, and do not rush.

3) Then practice the whole measure to beat one of the next measure, still playing one impulse.

4) Start impulse practice on any downbeat. You can say to yourself the fingerings of the right-hand patterns. In this way, you will train your mind to know the slight differences among the three patterns.

Minuet in F

Wolfgang Amadeus Mozart
KV 6, Minuet II

LITTLE FUNERAL MARCH

This funeral march was composed for "Del Signor Maestro Contrapunto." It was intended to be a joke, and Mozart wrote this when he was a grown man, probably for one of his *pianoforte* students. It was composed in Vienna, Austria, in 1784.

Characteristics of the Classical Era

Pieces in the Classical era use varied rhythms.

Notice the three recurring rhythms in this piece and tap them on the fallboard several times:

Dotted rhythms:

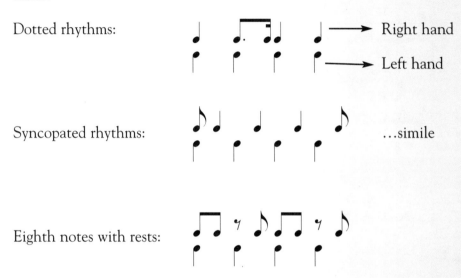

→ Right hand

→ Left hand

Syncopated rhythms:

...simile

Eighth notes with rests:

Silences/rests are just as important as the notes, so give them their full time value!

Practice Strategy

Bringing the piece to life musically:

This piece is a study in huge contrasts in regard to dynamics, touch, and style. Find the following musical attributes and mark them in your score (with a pencil!):

1) Which notes should be voiced over the others? (See Haydn's *Scherzo in F* for more information.) For example, in measures 5 and 6, is the top or lower line of the right hand more prominent? And what about measure 7? Circle these notes in your score.

2) Circle where the loudest and quietest phrases are. In order to make a real distinction between the *forte* and *piano*, play the *forte* phrases heavily and the *piano* phrases lightly.

3) Mark where you hear any *poco ritardando*.

4) Do you hear any phrase that is not marked *legato* in the score, but is interpreted as *legato* on the recording?

LITTLE FUNERAL MARCH

Wolfgang Amadeus Mozart
KV 453[a]

a) Optional chord may be substituted for a smaller hand.

MODERATO IN F MAJOR

This vivacious piece is part of the London Sketchbook Mozart composed during the time he and his sister were giving recital performances in England.

Practice Strategy

How to create clear passagework:

Bach's son, Carl Philipp Emanuel, who was also a famed composer, advised, "All difficulties in passage work should be mastered through repeated practice." (C.P.E. Bach, in his *Essay on the True Art of Playing Keyboard Instruments*)

In order to perform passagework that is even and clear, and that sparkles over the left-hand accompaniment, follow these basic practice strategies:

Start with "smart fingering." Use fingering that facilitates movement, and which fits the hand. Fingering is marked in the score to help you.

Isolate similar motives and practice them with a metronome, *a tempo*, hands separately. Listen to the clarity of sound and articulation. For example, practice all of the motives that look like this at least eight times in a row:

Upbeats to m. 1   Upbeats to m. 15

Then practice all of the two-note ascending motives that look like this:

m. 2   m. 4   m. 12   m. 16

Then practice all of the measures that have longer sixteenth-note and triplet patterns in them, such as:

m. 5-6 right hand   m. 11-13 left hand   m. 36-38 right hand

Isolate the measures that have double thirds. Practice slowly at first, and then up to tempo.

m. 20–21   m. 22–24

Isolate all embellishments. Practice hands together, without the ornaments, and then add them. Again, listen for clarity of sound and use "smart fingering."

Practice Strategy

Articulating wedges and staccatos:

Mozart used both forms of *staccato*. Notes with a wedge (▼) should be released instantly, while notes with a *staccato* have a little less resonance. An easy-to-remember guide when playing notes with *staccato* or wedge markings is the following:

1) A *staccato* note subtracts $\frac{1}{2}$ the value from the note.
2) A wedge, or *staccatissimo*, takes away $\frac{3}{4}$ of the value, so it is very short!

Listen to the difference between these two kinds of *staccato*.

The Kärtner Gate Theater, Vienna, 1825

Moderato in F major

Wolfgang Amadeus Mozart
KV Anh. 109[b], No. 1 (15[a])

(b) Optional trills: or

THE PIANOFORTE

Mozart played on all of the keyboard instruments of his time, and he especially liked the *pianoforte*. The instruments in the Classical era were made in Germany and Austria, and such names as Stein, Walter, and Streicher were famous for making these instruments. The *pianoforte* had only a five-octave keyboard range, but it was capable of producing both *crescendo* and *diminuendo* so there could be greater shading of dynamics as well as a fuller *forte*. This enabled the player to bring out the melodic line over a quieter accompanimental figure in the bass. The newly developed escapement action made it possible for the hammers to rebound instantly from the strings, thus allowing the performer to play in a *legato* fashion for the first time. This was in vast contrast to the harpsichord action during the Baroque era.

The action of this new keyboard instrument was quick and light, making a greater range of articulation possible for the performer. A new addition was a knee pedal instead of the foot pedals we know today. Mozart was extremely pleased with the new pedal device, as he wrote in one of his letters to his father dating from Germany on the 17-18th of October 1777.

> Stein has improved on the contrivance for exerting pressure by
> the knee. I can put it in action with the lightest touch, and when
> one slackens the knee-pressure a little there is no trace of an echo.[1]

The genre of opera was very important during the Classical era, and with the *pianoforte's* new *legato* capability, composers wrote for a more "singing" style that is called *cantabile*. Mozart learned the *cantabile* style of playing as a student of C.P.E. Bach, who had studied for a time in Italy. Mozart himself had the chance to travel to Italy when he was thirteen, further immersing himself in the *cantabile* style.

One of Mozart's *pianofortes*, made by Anton Walter of Vienna in 1783, is pictured below. Notice the simple construction of the instrument. You can see this keyboard instrument if you visit Mozart's home in Salzburg, Austria. Maybe someday you will play one of these pieces on Mozart's very own piano.

[1]Hans Mersmann, editor. <u>Letters of Wolfgang Amadeus Mozart</u>. Dover Publications, Inc., New York, New York, 1972, p. 37.

Mozart's *pianoforte*, made c.1783

ADAGIO IN C

This piece was written in Austria, for an instrument called a glass harmonica.
Mozart wrote it in 1791, the last year of his life. The glass harmonica had many
different vessels of varying sizes, filled with different amounts of water. The glasses
rotated on a spindle, and the musician would rub his fingers around the circular rim of
the glasses, obtaining a different note or tone from each one. The American Benjamin
Franklin is said to be one of the first inventors of this instrument.

Practice Strategy

Creating long phrases:

Shown below are the first twelve measures of the Adagio. Mozart's slurs do not indicate the
beginnings and ends of musical phrases. He used short slurs to indicate the articulation
instead. The first note of the slur should be marked, but not accented.

Longer slurs demonstrate the phrases. The phrases throughout this sensitive piece are two,
three, or four measures long. As you listen to the recording of this piece, mark the phrases
of varying length directly in your score.

Incorporating pedal:

Practice Strategy

This Adagio is greatly enhanced by the careful use of the pedal; the pedal creates an
overall *legato* that makes the piece very smooth, like the sounds emanating from a glass
harmonica. The pedal helps to avoid dryness of tone.

The pedal may be used to create a perfect *legato* in the
musical line. For example, in order to connect all of the
notes, play the D-F on beat two, and then depress the
pedal. Release the pedal as soon as you play the E-G.
Pedaling like this allows you to connect the notes even
when it is impossible to do so using only the fingers.

ADAGIO IN C

Wolfgang Amadeus Mozart
KV 356 (617ª)

(a) Pedal after the notes are played for a *legato* connection. Release the pedal where marked.

Mozart's birth house, Salzburg, Austria

PRESTO IN B FLAT MAJOR

This lively piece, written in 1765, is also part of the
London Sketchbook. The pieces in this notebook were
either for keyboard or sketches for orchestra.

**Characteristics
of the
Classical Era**

Musical characteristics of the era exemplified in this piece:

- ■ Varied rhythmic motives
- ■ Dynamic changes contribute to the overall expression of the piece
- ■ Use of binary form

**Practice
Strategy**

"Blocking" helps you to see and feel the patterns more readily than if you just try to
learn this piece note by note.

Play the circled patterns as blocked chords:

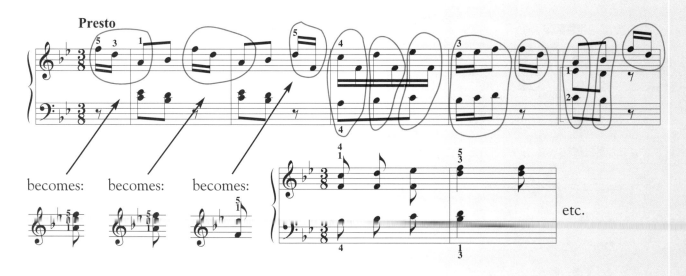

becomes: becomes: becomes:

etc.

Measures 9-10:

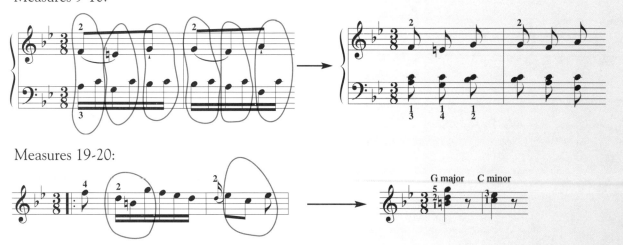

Measures 19-20:

Shaping the phrases:

Once you know the rhythms and the notes of this piece well, you are ready to think about the forward direction of the musical line. Every phrase has one high point, or musical goal. Circled below are a few examples of phrases with their musical goal. Play these, listening to the *crescendo* and *decrescendo* through the phrase. Then apply this strategy to all of the phrases in the piece.

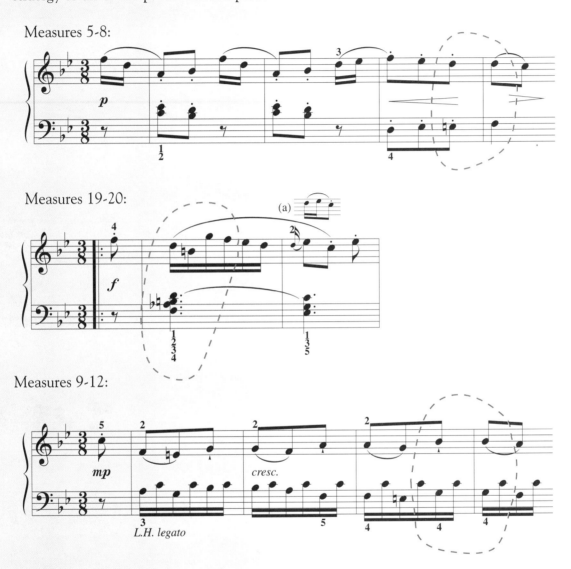

Measures 5-8:

Measures 19-20:

Measures 9-12:

This Presto should be played *secco*, which means dry. This kind of touch is very important in playing the faster works by Mozart.

PRESTO IN B FLAT MAJOR

Wolfgang Amadeus Mozart
KV Anh. 109ᵇ, No. 9 (15ᴵᴵ)

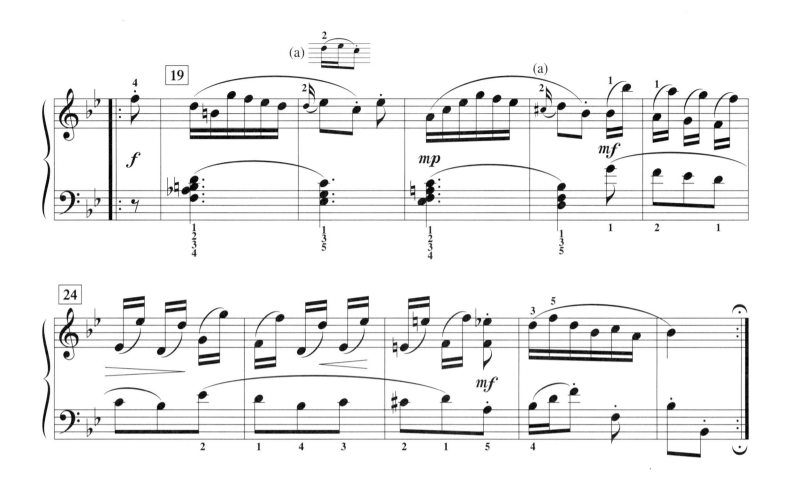

18th Century Salzburg, Austria

LUDWIG VAN BEETHOVEN

(1770–1827)

In 1787, Beethoven visited Vienna to study with Mozart. He remained in Vienna for only two weeks, traveling back to Bonn with the news of his mother's death. A year after Mozart died, in 1792, Beethoven moved permanently to Vienna in order to study with Haydn, who was then regarded as the greatest composer in all of Europe. Beethoven outfitted his new lodging with the essentials: "...wood, wig, coffee... overcoat, boots, shoes, piano-desk..."[1] He studied with Haydn until 1794, when Haydn left for London. He then continued his formal instruction with a teacher by the name of Johann Georg Albrechtsberger. Haydn and Mozart were undoubtedly two of the primary artistic influences on Beethoven's life. In 1800 he organized a concert of his own music and theirs.

Nature was an inspiration for Beethoven. He would take long walks in the country, keeping a sketchbook with him to write down musical ideas for compositions. When asked where his creative ideas came from, Beethoven replied:

> You will ask me where I take my ideas? That I cannot say with any
> degree of certainty; they come to me uninvited, directly or indirectly.
> I could almost grasp them in my hands, out in Nature's open, in the
> woods, during my promenades, in the silence of the night, at the
> earliest dawn. They are roused by moods which in the poet's case
> are transmuted into words, and in mine into tones, that sound, roar
> and storm until at last they take shape for me as notes.[2]

Society had changed by the time Beethoven came on the scene and it was easier to survive without a permanent position. Thus, Beethoven enjoyed a great deal of the personal liberty that neither Haydn nor Mozart had experienced. Noble patrons engaged in a delightful hobby — commissioning Beethoven to write music for special occasions and for special people in their families. By the age of thirty, Beethoven was considered the most outstanding composer of his day, and he could demand high fees. When offers were made to move and work in other European cities, three gentlemen of nobility in Vienna each paid Beethoven a salary to keep him there. His reputation was so great that every time Beethoven wrote a new piece, several publishers wanted to publish it. Before long, publishers began to approach him, asking him for new works for their companies.

Beethoven was known for being passionate and often moody. He was generous, but he could also be offensive and impulsive. He poured his emotions into his works, which was one reason why audiences were drawn to his music.

The piano in Beethoven's time continued to evolve from the *pianoforte* Mozart played. The Broadwood Piano Company of London, England, in 1818, developed a piano with a keyboard range of over six octaves and sent it to Beethoven. He wrote many of his finest piano pieces on this instrument.

In his late twenties, Beethoven began to lose his hearing. He continued to compose with the aid of rudimentary hearing devices, some of which you can see on display if you visit his childhood home in Bonn, Germany. As Beethoven became completely deaf, he lost more and more contact with others and retreated into himself. In 1801, he wrote:

> I must confess that I am living a miserable life. For almost two years I have
> ceased to attend any social functions, just because I find it impossible to say
> to people: I am deaf. If I had any other profession it would be easier, but in
> my profession it is a terrible handicap.[3]

Despite his deafness — the worst imaginable fate for a composer — he created some of the best music ever written and he is considered one of the greatest composers to have ever lived. His creative genius paved the way from the Classical era to the Romantic era, which was characterized by greater emotionality, because audiences experienced the intensity of his emotions when they heard his music. Over 20,000 people came to mourn the great composer at his funeral in Vienna. Beethoven's music touched the inner core of his fellow man, and generations of composers since have emulated and revered him.

His huge creative output included nine symphonies, thirty-two piano sonatas, five piano concertos, and sixteen string quartets. Beethoven catalogued his works by giving each set an "Opus" number. "Opus" is the Latin word for "work." Pieces he did not publish during his lifetime, found after his death, are listed as "WoO" numbers. "WoO" means, in German, "Werk ohne Opuszahl" (literally, "work without opus number").

[1] Barry Cooper, editor, Beethoven Compendium, London: Thames and Hudson, 1991, 14.

[2] Donald Jay Grout, editor, A History of Western Music, New York, New York: W.W. Norton and Company, Inc., 1973, 516.

[3] Stanley Sadie, ed, The New Grove Dictionary of Music and Musicians, second edition, Ludwig van Beethoven, London: Macmillan Publishers, 2001, 80.

Water-color of Beethoven's funeral procession in Vienna, 1827, by F. Stöber

GERMAN DANCE IN E FLAT MAJOR

This German Dance is from a collection titled *12 Deutsche Tänze,* written in 1800. Beethoven's first benefit concert in Vienna occurred in the same year and included premieres of his First Symphony and works by Haydn and Mozart. Since Beethoven taught many students, this set was probably used as teaching repertoire.

Characteristics of the Classical Era

Characteristics of the Classical era exemplified in this piece:

- Minuet and trio form
- Well-balanced and symmetrical phrases
- Use of *sforzandos* create the feeling of a dance and add character to the overall dynamic scheme

In order to make this piece feel like a dance, you can create longer, eight-measure phrases, feeling the forward motion of the melodic line. Below, the right-hand melody of the trio section is marked in four-bar phrases. When you play the piece, however, do not linger at the end of every four measures. Instead, keep going to make longer phrases. You can follow this same thought process for the A section.

Practice Strategy

Practicing *Alberti* basses:

A popular accompaniment pattern in the Classical era is the *Alberti* bass, named after the composer who devised it (see glossary).

1) Never reach with your fingers, but keep them in a rounded shape with a relaxed wrist and a knuckle bridge that is higher than the wrist.

2) When playing the fourth or fifth finger, transfer your arm weight to this part of the hand. You may wish to accent this finger, which will help you to transfer your arm weight to the thumb immediately afterward.

Title page from a piano edition of Beethoven's composition, *Wellington's Victory*

German Dance in E flat major

Ludwig van Beethoven
WoO 13, No. 9

ped. simile

Fine

BAGATELLE IN A MINOR

This piece is from a set of Bagatelles (short, light "trifles"). Composed between 1820–1822, these pieces were presented to a piano educator named Starke for a new piano teaching method. In these same years, Beethoven began to write his last three monumental piano sonatas.

Characteristics of the Classical Era

Homophonic texture:

Much of classical music has a *homophonic* texture. This means that chords in the left hand create harmony that support a melodic voice in the right hand. As you practice this piece, always listen for your right hand to be clearly heard over the left-hand waltz pattern.

"Smart" fingering:

Practice Strategy

Often pianists will experiment with different fingerings in order to find one that is right for their particular build and size. The opening phrase can easily be played with three *different* fingerings:

1)

2)

3)

In order to choose the one that is right for you, practice in the following ways:

1) Block the notes into chords or harmonic intervals, like this:

2) Play slowly with a strong sound several times.

3) Then, play the two-measure gesture quickly in order to feel it at a performance tempo.

When you are sure you have chosen the correct fingering, write it in your score and *use it all of the time!*

Practicing the melody in rhythms:

Practicing in different rhythms will help you to achieve absolute evenness and will help you build speed. With the metronome set at ♪ M.M. = 120, 144, and then 168, practice the first phrase in the following rhythms:

Practice Strategy

1   +   2   3   1   +   2   3   1   +   2   3

1   2   +   3   1   2   +   3   1   2   3

1 e + a 2 e + a 3 e + a 1 e + a 2 e + a 3

1 e + a 2 e + a 3 e + a 1 e + a 2 e + a 3

Remember, once you have chosen the fingering that suits you best, always use it!

Bagatelle in A minor

Ludwig van Beethoven
Op. 119, No. 9

(a) The lower A may be omitted if played by a smaller hand.

*Taken from the first edition, probably in Beethoven's own handwriting: *vivace assai ed un poco sentimentale*.

Vienna, circa 1760

ALLEMANDE IN A

This Allemande was composed in 1793. That year Beethoven
bought a gift of coffee and chocolate for Haydn and that same year
in America, George Washington was President!

**Characteristics
of the
Classical Era**

There is often a "contrast of mood."

In the Classical era, fluctuating moods are prevalent, whereas in the Baroque period, the
same mood permeates an entire piece.

Draw a line from the section in the left-hand column to the characteristics in the right-
hand column which best describe it.

<u>**A and B sections**</u>   <u>**mood characteristics of sections**</u>

A section

marked and determined

elegant and delicate

B section

light and graceful

steadfast and confident

**Practice
Strategy**

Practicing arpeggios: Practice arpeggios in these three ways to be successful:
1) "Impulse" practicing
2) Practicing in rhythms (see the *Bagatelle* in this volume, page 70)
3) Practicing up and down, without stopping, accenting different notes.

The minuet section is graceful and lively, because of its continuous sixteenth-note
patterns. "Impulse" practicing will help to make this section clean and clear. An
"impulse" is when you divide a long passage into short segments. First, practice going to
beat two of measure one (impulse 1 below). Repeat until it is easy and feels natural.
Then practice playing to the third beat of the measure (impulse 2 below), and then to
the last note of the measure (impulse 3). Finally, practice to the next downbeat (impulse
4). Repeat until clear and even, always listening to yourself. By using these steps, you will
be able to play *leggiero*, which means lightly and rapidly.

Impulse 1    Impulse 2

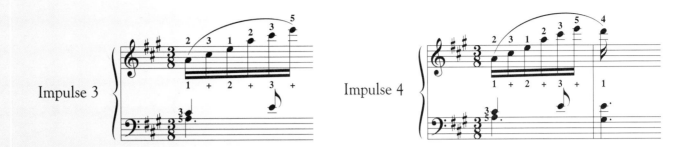

Impulse 3   Impulse 4

Practice Strategy

Regrouping:

Once you have learned this piece, use a "regrouping" practice strategy. Rather than starting at the beginning of a phrase, regroup the phrase so that it begins at different places. For example, begin playing in the *middle* of a measure and play until you reach a downbeat.

Middle of measure one to the downbeat of measure 3:

Middle of measure three to the downbeat of measure 5:

While you play these repeatedly, have the last note of the group end on an accent, and then lift your wrist as you lift off the key. This "regrouping" strategy makes your fingers comfortable to start at any place in the phrase, which will help you to gain necessary confidence for an effective performance.

ALLEMANDE IN A

Ludwig van Beethoven
WoO 81

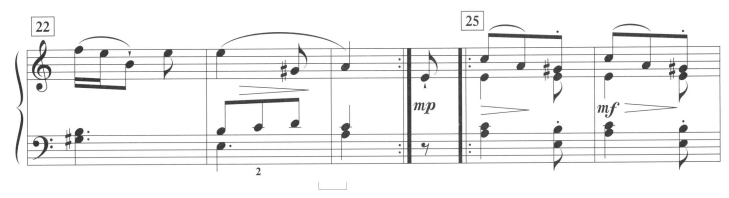

D.C. al Fine

*Pedal until the downbeat.

WALTZ IN E FLAT MAJOR

The Waltz in E Flat Major was written in 1824, the same year Beethoven's Symphony No. 9 was premiered in Vienna, Austria, as well as in London, England. At the end of the concert in London, Beethoven had to be turned to face the enthusiastically applauding audience because by this time Beethoven was so deaf he had not noticed their clapping. Imagine what a mind he had, to write his great Symphony No. 9 without being able to hear!

**Characteristics
of the
Classical Era**

The emergence of the waltz:

In order to create the feeling of this dance form, we must become acquainted with what a waltz is. A waltz is a dance in triple time, slow or fast, with one strong beat per bar. The waltz developed from the "German Dance" written by Viennese composers, and the waltz became widely popular throughout Europe in the late 18th century.

**Practice
Strategy**

Practicing a waltz bass:

1) To learn the notes correctly, use the "play-prepare" practice strategy. Play all of the notes of the measure as a blocked chord. Then, move your hand and silently *prepare* your fingers over the notes of the next measure (circled below).

Prepare your fingers each time.

Only when you know that your fingers are on the correct keys should you actually *play* the notes. Use this strategy for every measure.

2) To feel one beat per bar, drop into the downbeat with your left hand and then immediately lift off and move to the second beat. On the second and third beats, play lightly and on your fingertips!

**Practice
Strategy**

Practicing with the metronome:

The metronome was patented by John Maelzel in 1815. Beethoven enthusiastically used this device to set tempo markings for his larger works.

Using the metronome helps to develop an inner sense of pulse and is one of the best ways to gradually increase the tempo without losing control.

With the metronome on, practice hands separately first, then hands together. It's a good idea to sometimes stop on the downbeats to make sure you are lining up your playing with the tick of the metronome.

Once you have practiced with the metronome and know that you can play the waltz evenly and steadily, you can turn off the metronome and play with more freedom and *rubato*. Listen to the recording and write in your score where this sense of freedom takes place.

Using imagery to create a successful performance:

At times, creating a story in your mind will help you to play the piece with more color and spontaneity.

The trio section might depict village bells in the Austrian countryside. The pedal is to be held for eight measures, as we imagine the bells sounding from afar.

Listen to the recording and create a story for the A section, and then for the whole piece.

A pencil drawing of Beethoven's birthplace in Bonn, Germany, by R. Beissel

WALTZ IN E FLAT MAJOR

Ludwig van Beethoven
WoO 84

(a) A section: Pedal only on the downbeats, except where indicated.

(b) These sixteenth notes are played before the beat, as grace notes.

MINUET IN C MAJOR

In 1795, Beethoven composed his six minuets of WoO10. This is the first of the set. The same year, Beethoven dedicated his first piano sonatas (Op. 2) to Haydn, who had been his teacher for a brief time.

Characteristics of the Classical Era

Straightforward harmonies are typically used in classical pieces.

Beethoven was a master at creating compositions that utilize strong tonic (I) to dominant (V) harmonies.

Below is the A section of this Minuet and Trio. Circle the measures that are dominant (V) or (V7) harmony.

Most of the minuet has been labeled for you below. Then, listen to the recording and notice how the tonic phrases are more grounded while the dominant phrases sound less stable and lead back to tonic.

Playing sixteenth notes evenly:

Here are two ways to succeed:

1) Count out loud and subdivide the sixteenth notes as well as the following quarter notes, like this:

This will keep you from rushing, while still feeling the forward direction of the line.

2) On the first note of every sixteenth-note motive, move your wrist by freely dropping it below your knuckle bridge. Listen carefully, making sure that all of the sixteenth notes are played clearly together. Do not tense your muscles! On the last note of the motive, roll up on your fingertips moving toward the fallboard, and let your wrists follow the line of motion. This motion is not large and exaggerated, but natural. Once this gesture becomes effortless, you will hear a perky and clean melodic gesture.

Finding places to relax for better facility:

This piece needs to sound dramatic and heroic. This means that it is necessary for you to have some tension in your muscles. The important thing is to learn how and when to release this tension. There are places in the music where you can make yourself be aware of the importance of relaxing your arms and wrists. To practice, play the following phrases, and when you reach the places that are checked, drop your arms loosely to your sides. This strategy will help you become aware of the need for tension and relaxation in the same muscles.

MINUET IN C MAJOR

Ludwig van Beethoven
WoO 10, No. 1

*Depress the pedal briefly.

Fine

*If desired, you may pedal lightly (1/2 pedal) from every third beat to every downbeat in measures 17-24.

(a) The grace note is played *before* the beat.

KLAVIERSTÜCK
Für Elise

(Translated, Für Elise means "For Elise")
This piece was written on April 27, 1810 for a woman
named Therese Malfatti. Very little is known about her,
even though this piece is very famous.

**Characteristics
of the
Classical Era**

Rondo form:

A new form used often in the Classical era was called the "rondo." In rondo form, the main theme is heard several times throughout a work, but it is separated by contrasting themes.

A	B	A	C	A
Main theme	contrasting theme	main theme	another contrasting theme	main theme
m. 1-22	pick-ups to m. 23-38	pick-up to m. 38-59	m. 59-82	m. 82-end

A theme   **B theme**

C theme

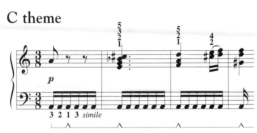

Mark this form directly into your score.

What key are all of the A sections in? (such as measures 1-22): _____

The B section (starting with the pick ups to measure 23) is in F major, which is the sixth scale degree of the original key. Harmonic relationships of a third became common in the Romantic era as composers looked for new and different ways to broaden the harmonic language set in the Classical era. Beethoven, the innovator, expanded the traditional harmonic language, experimented with form, and expanded the orchestra. All of these changes set the stage for the Romantic era to follow the Classical era.

Contrast of mood:

This piece is deceptively challenging because of its abrupt changes in mood. Not only do the emotions change in each section of the piece, but so do the technical challenges. The thirty-second notes in measures 30-35 of the B section must be the same tempo as the rest of the section. It is important to begin the B section at a tempo that you can control throughout.

Measures 22-31:

At the return of the A section, the tempo must be the same as at the beginning of the piece.

Using the *una corda* pedal

Practice Strategy

In order to create a significant change in mood and to play *pianissimo*, you may use the *una corda* pedal. The *una corda* pedal not only makes the tone softer, but also changes the sound. The *una corda* pedal makes the sound more mellow and transparent. These changes in color help to create the mood changes that are so important in Classical era repertoire.

Una corda, in Italian, means "one string." *The *una corda* shifts the piano action so that the hammer strikes one string instead of three. *Tre corde* (3 strings) means to release the *una corda* pedal, allowing the hammer to strike all three strings. The *una corda* pedal is the pedal on the left and you should play it with your left foot, so that your right foot can still push the right *damper* pedal as needed.

Listen to the recording of *Für Elise* and see if you can tell when the *una corda* pedal is used.

* On upright pianos, the hammers are brought closer to the strings.

KLAVIERSTÜCK
Für Elise

Ludwig van Beethoven
WoO 59

*The contrasting B section may be played *meno mosso*.

**R.H. *legato* in measures 30-36.

*Measures 77-83: The *una corda* pedal may be used.

MINUET IN D MAJOR

This piece is the fifth minuet of Beethoven's WoO10 set, written in 1795. The same year, in France, the famous Paris music conservatory was founded. Four years earlier, the first edition of the Encyclopedia Britannica was published in Britain.

Characteristics of the Classical Era

The classical orchestra became established.

The popularity of writing symphonies for orchestras increased, and during the Classical era the genre went through many changes.

The classical symphony usually has these characteristics:

1) Four sections, or movements, with a pause between each movement.

2) Each movement has a specific "plan," or "form."
First movement – "sonata form" (see page 32)
Second movement – slow and lyrical
Third movement – a minuet and trio form that gives the feeling of relaxation
Fourth movement – light, energetic, spirited, and swiftly moving

3) Small orchestras, consisting of a string section, limited woodwind and brass, and a timpanist.

Although classical orchestras were small compared to the orchestras we know today, this Minuet is "orchestral" in nature, because of the large contrast in mood, dynamics, rhythm, and melodic material.

Practice Strategy

Thinking orchestrally to bring this piece to life:

Imagine that you are Beethoven and you are planning to "orchestrate" this piano piece, meaning you want to write it so that it can be played by an orchestra. Think about which instrument(s) would create a dramatic sound for the opening theme, and which instrument(s) could float above other instruments that are quietly playing the harmonic framework in the trio section. You can use the recording to help you decide.

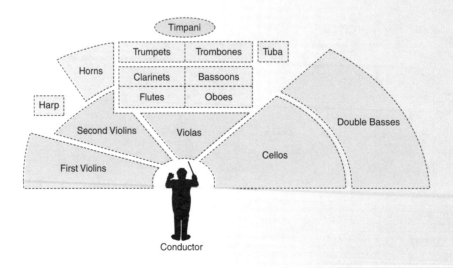

Practice Strategy

Main theme: Could it be played by: 1) the full orchestra, 2) just the brass, 3) just the winds?_____

Which instruments could be added to play the *sforzandi*?_____

Which instruments could play the melody in the trio section? (flute, oboe, bassoon, clarinet)

_____

Which instruments could play this middle part? (in color)_____

MINUET IN D MAJOR

Ludwig van Beethoven
WoO 10, No. 5

*Eighth notes should be played *staccato*.

Beethoven portrait by J.C. Stieler, 1819

SIX VARIATIONS ON A SWISS SONG

This Theme and Variations was composed in 1790, the same year that Joseph II, Emperor of the Austro-Hungarian empire, died. This influential emperor ruled over a large portion of Europe; and Haydn, Mozart, and Beethoven all lived under his laws. In the same year, Haydn came to visit Beethoven in Bonn, Germany.

Characteristics of the Classical Era

Characteristics of the Classical era exemplified in this piece:

- Melodies that are elegant, graceful, and easy to sing
- The newly popular form of a theme followed by several variations of the theme (called "theme and variations")
- Rhythmic motives are varied
- Dynamic changes contributing to the overall expression of the piece

Practice Strategy

Playing *portato* articulations:

The term *portato* tells us to play the notes within a slur with a slight articulation. Imagine that you are combining two techniques to create a wonderful new effect. Note that the *portato* articulation is identified by *staccato* marks within a slur, showing us that it is indeed two different techniques combined.

Practice Strategy

Listening to the interpretation on the recording:

Answer the following questions:

1) Which variation has the most dotted rhythms in the harmony? _____

2) Which variation is comprised of triplet patterns? _____

3) Which variations are the most gentle? _____

4) Which variations are the most bold and dramatic? _____

5) Which variation has melody and accompaniment within the *same* hand? _____

6) Listening to variation IV, add your own phrasing marks to the score.

Listen carefully to the rise and fall of the melody, and where the phrase goals are.

Where does the pianist lift her hands and let the music "breathe"?

As you play each variation, create a different personality for each one. This will help the piece come to life for you and for the audience.

SIX VARIATIONS ON A SWISS SONG

Ludwig van Beethoven
WoO 64

Thema con Variazioni (Schweizer Lied)
Andante con moto (♩ = M.M. 132-138)

N.B. The longer slurs have been added to show the shape of the phrase.

Var. II

Var. III Minore (♩ = M.M. 100-116)

Var. IV Maggiore (♩ = M.M. 132-138)

Var. V (♩ = M.M. 108-112)

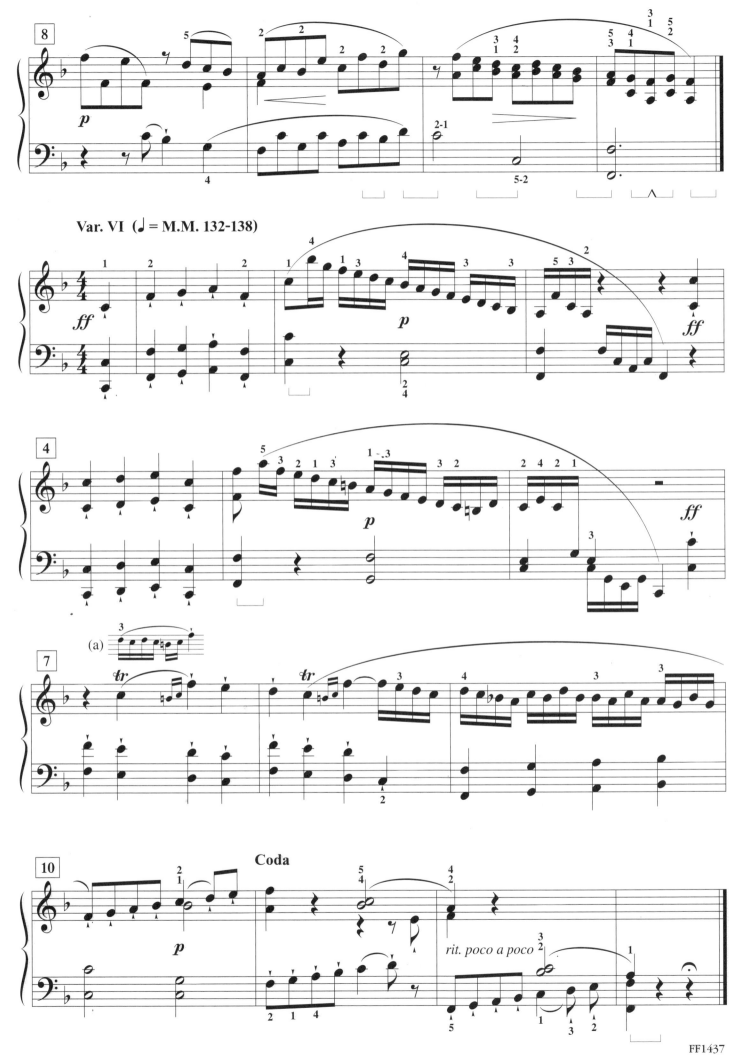

Volume Two – Repertoire with their Sources

Sources consulted for this edition:

Haydn, Joseph. <u>Pieces for a Musical Clock.</u> Bärenreiter, Kassel: Basel: London, 1954.

Haydn, Joseph. <u>Joseph Haydn Werke.</u> G. Henle Verlag, München, 1995.

Haydn, Joseph. <u>The Complete Piano Works of Haydn.</u> Könemann Music,
    Budapest, Hungary, 1997.

Mozart, Wolfgang Amadeus. <u>Neue Ausgabe sämtlicher Werke.</u> Bärenreiter edition,
    Kassel: Basel: London, 1991.

Beethoven, Ludwig, van. <u>Ludwig van Beethoven Werke.</u> G. Henle Verlag,
    München, 1971.

Beethoven, Ludwig, van. <u>Ludwig van Beethoven's Werke.</u> Verlag von Breitkopf &
    Härtel. Leipzig, 1949.

Beethoven, Ludwig van. <u>Kleinere Klavierwerke.</u> Könemann Music, Budapest,
    Hungary, 1999.

GLOSSARY OF MUSICAL TERMS

Tempo markings

Presto	*Allegro*	*Moderato*	*Andante*
Quick, fast	cheerful, bright, faster than *allegretto*	a moderate tempo	walking tempo
Prestissimo is even faster			

Accompaniment – a musical background for a principal part. The background may be the left hand of a keyboard composition or orchestral background for a solo instrument. The accompaniment provides harmony for the melody.

Alberti bass – an accompaniment pattern consisting of broken chords with notes in the pattern: lowest, highest, middle, highest. This bass-line pattern was devised by an Italian composer named Domenico Alberti (1710–1740). Fourteen of his harpsichord sonatas have survived in their entirety.

Allemande – in the late 18th century, this term applied to a dance in triple meter.

Appoggiatura – an upper neighbor note that is played on the beat and stressed before it resolves to a principal note. From the Italian word, *appoggiare*, which means, "to lean."

Arpeggio – an Italian word meaning, "harp-like." The sounding of successive notes of a chord, rather than all at once.

a tempo – return to the regular tempo, especially after a *ritardando (rit.)*.

Authentic cadence – a closing formula, usually two chords, that move from the dominant chord (V) to the tonic (I, i).

Binary form – a piece built in two parts (AB); the first part usually ends on the dominant (V) but sometimes on the tonic (I, i). Both parts are usually marked to be repeated before going on.

Bridge – melodic material that brings together two themes or two parts of a piece.

Embellishment – also called ornamentation. The way composers fill out or decorate the texture, making the sound more grand.

Homophonic texture – a melody supported by harmonies; the melodic voice is often in the right hand with chords in the left hand creating the harmony. It can be done the other way around, melody in the left hand and chords above.

Legatissimo – is the superlative for the term, *legato,* meaning smooth or grouped.

Leggeremente – very lightly, delicately and rapidly. (Beethoven spelled the word *leggiermente* in his Allemande in A.)

Minuet and Trio – a three-part musical form that combines an elegant dance, the main minuet, in triple meter, with a contrasting "little" minuet (called the trio). The trio is in the same meter and key, but may be in minor instead of major, for contrast. The first minuet comes back after the trio section to complete a three-part composition. Note: both the main minuet and the trio minuet will themselves be little binary forms (see binary form above).

Motive – a short melodic or rhythmic pattern (a few pitches) from which a full melodic and rhythmic phrase may grow.

(N.B.) Nota Bene – a Latin phrase meaning, "mark well." Used to point out something important.

Phrase goal – the place toward which the music naturally moves, as in spoken sentences, where one word has slightly more emphasis or volume than others. Let your ear be your guide and follow this rise of melody towards a goal. After arrival at its goal, the phrase naturally tapers.

Portato – an articulation identified by *staccato* marks within a slur, showing us that two different techniques are combined.

Rondo form – a piece or movement in which a main theme is heard several times throughout a work but is separated by contrasting themes or material. A B A C A, or A B A C A D A, etc.

Rounded Binary – a piece in regular binary form, with one difference: the opening tune of the A section returns within the B section to lead back to a nice ("rounded") conclusion for the piece.

Rubato – the Italian word for "stolen." To stretch or broaden the tempo. However, the time taken can be made up within the same phrase or shortly thereafter.

Scherzo – an Italian word for joke. Beethoven was the first to replace the minuet for the quickly-paced *scherzo* in his sonatas, symphonies, and chamber works.

Sforzando – an Italian term (abbreviated *sf*), which means to create a sudden, strong accent on a note or chord.

Sonata form – a newly established three-part form during the Classical era. The main theme or themes are heard in the exposition. These themes are changed during the development section, and then in the last section, the recapitulation, the main theme or themes return. Sonata form is used as the first movement of sonatas, symphonies, etc. For a complete definition, refer to *The FJH Classic Music Dictionary,* by Edwin McLean.

Theme and variations – a main melody that is then transformed melodically, harmonically, or rhythmically.

Trill – an ornament consisting of a repetitive alternation of a note with the note a whole or half step above it. The ornament usually begins above the principal note in the Baroque and Classical eras.

Waltz – a dance in triple time, slow or fast, with one beat to the bar. It first appeared in the late 18th century as a development from the "German Dances." The waltz was developed primarily by Viennese composers.